C01GDB390

Behold

Behold

Tom Dempster/Kathryn Timpany

KYKLOS Books
Sioux Falls, SD

Frontis Piece

the last words of Moses

The last words of Moses – Lake Sharpe, South Dakota

copyright 2009 by Tom Dempster
copyright 2009 by Kathryn Timpany

Library of Congress Control Number: 2009905348

ISB #978-0-615-28737-9

Acknowledgements

For those who have taken time to read and view our work, for those those have gone before us who have opened our souls, for those family, friends, and colleagues who have encouraged us to proceed, we offer our deepest gratitude.

Tom Dempster
Kathryn Timpany

Forward from the photographer

Two years ago I delivered photographs I was assembling for a calendar to my friend and minister, Kathy Timpany. She looked at me point blank and said, "So you're a photographer, huh?" "I am," I responded. "Well, I'm a poet. Why don't we publish a book?" she challenged. I began to submit photographs to her. To those that moved her, she would bequeath a poem. *Behold* is a result of that collaboration.

The prairie is a backdrop out of which sky and light and color are beheld as their beauty and drama unfold. As the earth turns into the sun, the images I come upon are there only that instant, never again to be. It is as if the image floats within the shell of an egg. Sometimes, I hold my breath hoping it will not shatter. When I walk within it I know it will soon vanish. Sometimes, it evaporates. But sometimes, I capture it.

Photographing people? Though perhaps as ephemeral as a landscape, a lock into another's eyes lasts an eternity. It is instinctive, open, trusting, and vulnerable. I never ask if I can take someone's portrait. And only three times have I been waved away – once in Denmark, in Syria, and in South Dakota.

When Kathy sees a photographic image, it becomes a musical score for her. From that score she finds lyrics, story and meaning. In the end, it is the photographer's joy to see, but it is the poet who teaches us the significance of what is seen.

Kathy sees the image of children standing on a threshold and paints them with stories we all remember from childhood. She inhales what I see and uses words to paint deeper, more personal, and more universal images.

Whether cowboys or monks, shikaras or South Dakota bridges, the Taj Mahal or the capital dome in Pierre, the Ganges or the Missouri, a freckle-faced brother and sister or kadhi-cotton-wrapped men, whether a yellow splash of Lord Vishnu or a tuba player in New York with an ace of spades in his bandana, these photographs and their poems celebrate our mysterious and rich lives and draw us into the community of the human spirit.

Forward from the poet

I am a poet. I hear sounds in my head that express experiences and emotions, and I use words to distill them into small fragments that can be held and pondered for a few moments at a time. All my life, I have written poetry to express what clamors to come out of me and take shape before me so that I can hear and see what I feel.

When I first saw Tom's photographs, I knew that he used the eye of his camera in the same way I used words. I knew that he understood what it meant to encounter the soul of someone or something. You have to pay very close attention, because brief glimpses of the magnificence that lies beneath the surface of all life come and go as if by whim. I knew that mystery and wonderment were the source of his vitality, as they are mine.

When Tom and I began to dream of a book, we first considered that we would approach it in two ways: Tom would read some of my poems and see if there were photographs that would illustrate them, and I would look at his photos and see if there were poems I had written that could become their captions.

What happened instead is one of the most satisfying creative processes I have ever experienced. I looked at his photographs, and they spoke to me as if they had a voice of their own. A tree in the mist spoke of marriage. Children told me what was on their hearts. Cultures crossed and melded together as a gathering of merchants in India spoke in the voices of Norwegian immigrants in Dakota Territory. Cowpokes sang songs as they clip-clopped along under the wide western sky. Sprays and vapors of water sang of sorrow and transcendence. Light spoke for itself, and there were almost no words sufficient to translate its lessons.

In most cases, the poems that accompany the photographs were written after sitting and letting them speak to me. I simply took dictation in the end. But in a few cases, a poem that I had already written seemed to fit itself to Tom's work, even though he would tell you that until he read what I had written, he had never thought of his photograph quite in that way before.

We invite you to immerse yourself in our work and see if something happens to you that will allow you the same, deep pleasure that we have known in creating this book. We hope to encourage you to see and hear something that has been there all along, but that you have not noticed before. And when you do, we would be delighted if you would find your own form to express in some small way the magnificence of the world that is our common home.

Dedication

for Tim, who taught me to see

for Patti, who loves

the last words of Moses

When you've come this far,

and it's taken this long,

and more times

than you'll ever want to remember

you were more than certain

you would never make it,

even though

the one you were listening to

has never once let you down,

not once,

and you finally arrive,

and – oh! – it is this! –

not only flowing with milk and honey

as you were promised,

but also offering a lush soft breast

on which to lay your weariness

and warring madness,

there is only one thing you can do.

Learn to touch

without bruising

for once in your life.

fear not

Walk on the water.

Go ahead.

I am not a ghost, long dead.

I make no magic,

ply no trade.

I want nothing.

Afraid, you linger.

Missing the clear light,

you are still lost in night.

Your feet

have lost the feel

of clean, of free.

But see! I walk,

glistening.

Go on,

I see you there,

waiting for your courage.

I see you there,

waiting.

joy to the world

Oh-h-h!

Oh, my!

Oh-my-o-my-o-my!

The light!

I see it after all!

The light,

it tickles my ribs!

My toes are dancing!

Well, they are!

I'll never be able

to sit still after this.

Never!

Who thought

it would be like this,

the light,

the end of night,

the end of banishment

behind bars,

the end of dark.

Oh! I see –

this is what

the defeat of evil

looks like!

I never thought

it would look like this!

Never in a thousand years!

Oh-h-h-h, my!

marriage

Are you two,

or are you one?

Did you spring from the same seed,

or were you companions

from before the dawn of time,

wanting merely

to be near until dusk?

It is clear

you drink from the same cup,

inhabit the same side of the road.

It is also clear

you know what sorrow is,

have broken under the burden

of too much wind,

or fire, or ice.

Someone has tended you with care,

mowed more around you

than they needed to.

Smoothed space enough

to wander in,

ponder who it is you are,

long for what it is you know.

Make sure you can be seen,

touched.

Someone has carved your name

into your common root,

just there beneath the tall grass

damp with dew and tears.

invitation

I see you have been

used to working a month at a time,

haggling for your pay,

rasping at the fish

as if they could hear you

and might quake,

flee into your net.

I see you think

you can startle them

with blood-color,

or do you just like its vibrancy,

its ruthless optimistic shout?

Well, come here then.

I have a better offer for you.

Come on,

if you can hold that still,

hold my gaze that long,

be that unashamed,

then you are the man for me.

If you like red that much,

then let me tell you

about work

that will last a lifetime,

and never run cold or gray.

dow jones average

The market
can make you crazy
with its secrets
and its mysteries.
Someone usually knows
what's going on,
and gets all the attention,
but if you are waiting
for oracles that will send you
to a different sphere,
you can wait a lifetime
and never make it,
and if you are wanting
to know who to trust,
look somewhere else.
But if you simply
like to drool and dance,
come on in.

norwegian bachelor farmers

They come in off the fields,

off their tractors,

in their new pick-ups

with the gleaming wheels.

They come to the table at the café

to brag and jibe,

to be as close as they know how to be.

They wear the same sweaters

year after year,

the ones their mothers made for their fathers

from ancient patterns

from the old country.

They know when to glare

and when to smile,

and have no pity on you

if you do not.

The harvest has been good this year,

very good.

It would be a mistake

to ask them how good,

to ask them how much

that new pick-up cost.

It would also be a mistake to think

that the first one who sold to the co-op

will be the last one standing

when the day is done.

best seats in the house

We've been here since last night,

braving the cold,

and then the slurs.   What they don't know,

The ticket office will open soon,   and seem so slow to learn

so they say.   is this:

                                        we'll wait as long as it takes

Our brothers told us not do this.   for a seat in the assembly.

We might get hurt,   As long as it takes.

worse yet, ignored.

They refused to wait with us.

cain's curse

Well, what did you expect?

I was the first born after all!

I had the land,

had planted my flag in it,

my seed in it.

Why would he get mad?

All I wanted

was my rightful place,

the favor due me.

If it was anybody's fault,

it was his, not mine!

Shoved out into the wilds,

only one cup and a bandanna

and a silly little pocket knife

in my ragged little pocket,

only that much,

and thieves and jackals all around.

And I am supposed to survive like this?

Well, am I?!

The other day I met a man.

He stopped in his tracks,

stared at me.

I got ready,

got ready to kill again,

or die trying.

But he just stared a long time.

Then walked on by.

Turned,

and called over his shoulder,

you should take a look at yourself.

I finally got a chance to,

in the shiny little bangle she dropped

when she left at dawn.

I am beautiful!

upriver

I have seen you here before,

on your way somewhere,

as I am.

I love these hills!

I love the way

they lie against the pale sky,

like clean sheets

dropped on the bed,

waiting to be smoothed.

I love to climb

to the crest of them,

and look out over the world.

This place is nice.

I am just resting here awhile,

here in the cool shade of columns.

Yes, you may.

Must kneel here beside me,

fold your hands like this.

This part isn't hard,

not hard at all.

It's what lies ahead

that will take your breath away.

git along little dogies

The cowboy's art
is all in the wrist,
like everything else
that demands finesse.

His sorrel mare,
on the other hand,
has fixed an eye
on the rolling land.

Easy in the saddle,
neither least nor best,
this eye-hand coordination's
what won the west.

genesis

The rock was as old as time,

as old as thought,

one billion, eight million years old.

It was the rock

that was fashioned on the third day,

standing up out of the gathered waters,

called *good*.

When we stood upon it,

you leaned into me,

and I into you,

for balance.

Your hands blessed flesh

that was a mere fifty-six years old,

and already fading

like the grass,

with something like steadfast love.

Downstream

a man cast a line

over the rippling water.

The light caught it,

caused it to shimmer gold,

and it too was *good*.

When he pulled the heaving trout

up and out

into the breathing air,

we smiled.

Over the sound of rippling waters,

he heard our accolades,

and held the fish higher.

Knowing we were watching,

he took great care

in all that followed after.

He didn't see us turn away.

Perhaps he kept the fish,

perhaps not.

As for me,

I shall keep

the warmth of you

forever,

and call it *holy*.

cup of life

Think of some things that are wet.

Dripping rain

slaking long drought.

Ocean spray.

Batter before it is baked.

Wine clinging

to the inside of communion cups.

Dew on the underside of leaves.

The roofs of caves.

Drinks that ooze

out from other things:

milk, juice,

malt, gravy.

The insides of mouths.

Life, when liquid,

begins beneath the crust

where air has not brushed it

with kissed lips of warm.

It is generous there.

Nothing ceases there.

Everflowing streams

emerge there.

Seeds and babies and ideas

begin there.

The word *love*

is formed there,

out of mist.

There are big words for this:

generosity, grace,

voluptuous, undulate.

There are pools that form.

There is something plump

that comes of it all.

Think of some things that are wet.

Drink them.

Now you are home.

Here. With me.

Drenched to the bone

with life.

At last.

Drink, drink, drink.

the best revenge

Build a bridge.

Wait for the sun to go down.

Take a deep breath.

Do it again.

Now start walking.

Don't stop

until you get to the other side.

Have a good life.

adam and eve

The curve of their hips

as they lie in repose afterward

reminds them of beloved hills

whose undulations rise

one after the other

beneath the wide sky's imitation

of liberating light.

Earlier it was other things

they thought about.

Spirals, geodes, horizons.

The way something round

looks fuller in the slant of dawn.

The gentleness of feathers

and whispers,

the scant hint of infinity within.

They understand now

what it means

that stones can be given voice

if all others fall silent.

They understand

that sometimes

it takes something astonishing

to get the attention of little gods,

something like birth

in the midst of death,

something fluid

and infinitely replenishable.

And so they lie still

and look at their hips

which are like hills,

and breathe in and out,

in and out,

in and out.

after armageddon

Think of me as rising if you must.

Remember warm yeast yearning,

working its way inside your nose

where it can be inhaled ravenously.

Or think of kites

whipping themselves silly,

dervished with sheer delight.

Or if you wish,

think of the pulsing arches

of ceilings in cathedrals

or capitals or chambered nautili,

bending your neck backward

so your eyes can find

infinity's vanishing point

in the light that lies behind them.

It doesn't even matter

if you think of me

as going up into the clouds

and staying there.

Be sure, though, to remember this:

I blessed you.

I opened your arms

wider than I ever had before,

and I blessed you.

Remember what it felt like

to brim with joy,

to be so bursting with blessing

that you couldn't

get to the temple fast enough,

and you couldn't stop acting

as if you were the one

who was lighter than air.

Then go ahead.

Think of me as rising,

right before your very eyes.

the way back

Go ahead. Mark it.
Use all your precision
and all your skill.
Lend it light.
Remember the way
it looks over your shoulder
as you move on down the road,
as you move on out
into the world,
as you claim your urgent future.

Just don't think
you can ever go back again.
Nothing will be the same.
Not even the thing
you thought could never change,
that great languid lap
upon which you once sat,
small and frightened,
as the night wind
roared around your ears
and the howl of death
echoed in its shattered wake.

Let your memory suffice.
It will be enough some day,
some day
when you are done
with walking.

i am the light

The morning light rises
like a dream wanting to be seen.
Some say that will be the end of it,
daring to declare itself that way,
lay itself out to be pelted
by the cynics and the cowards
and the dull of heart.

But light.
There has never
been a morning without it,
it is that steady,
that sure of itself.
Here and there
it even appears as a rainbow.
And when it does
things that are strapped down move.
Things that are settled
tremble and vanish like ghosts.

When dreams come true
you can be both safe
and astonished
all at once.

You shall see.
You shall see.

here i am

Afterward,
Sarah went out
to see for herself.
The altar lay bare.
No bones were found on it,
nor any blood,
nor any ashy, charcoal scar.
No sign that anyone
had thought of death,
let alone
the one who breathed
as she breathed,
night after night,
the one whose barren loins
she claimed for her own.
No sign of his great ardor,
greater ache.

Back home
the boy played
all jolly and full
of whistling once again,
all forgetful and fascinated
by the intricacies
he could hold in his hands
while he pondered
his own emerging power.

She stood a moment
longer than she needed to,
and her shut eyes
leaked love.

lux aeterna

There is light in your fingertips.

How does it get there?

Do you draw it up

from some core of glory

deep inside you?

Does it reside in the place

the melismas do,

the ones Bach hears

that none of the rest of us can hear

until he sings them?

You touch me,

and I am warm with it.

An aura grows.

Something like cumulus clouds

floats there in the place

that I have looked

for the best of myself

all my life long.

This comes through you,

to you from someplace else,

doesn't it?

What do you call it,

this light?

The light comes from you

and vibrates here,

hums here.

Becomes here

some kind of song.

How does this happen,

this turning of light

into the music of the spheres?

How does it feel

there in your fingertips?

How does it feel

when you lay it

lightly upon my life?

The light.

Can you teach the lost

to see with it

the way you have taught me

how to fly?

Well, can you?

*old
married
love*

Gradually,

the way one wisp of cirrus clouds

finds itself filling the sky

with a gauzy sheen,

the way water from an an open tap

overflows its basin

and wets the floor of the world,

the way a whiff of smoke

rises into the memory

of everyone who breathes,

old married love

moves from the poetic,

not, as some would say,

to the pedantic,

but slipping into ordinary things,

illuminating the core of them

the way night light does

when it slips between cloud cover

and snow cover, becomes –

ah! see! – becomes – oh! –

poetry in motion.

Or at least,

that is what has happened

to you and me,

transfigured as we are

by stars and shine,

by daring to climb

all the way up

to the top of the hill

that drew our eyes

the first time we bothered

to look for something

beyond our meager selves,

our impoverished imaginations.

Who knew

we could shimmer like this?

Who knew

we could glow as we burned,

grime turning to glory,

ash back into fire?

Who knew

we could breathe in smoke

and not choke,

but rise

as if the incense of it

could take us

all the way to paradise?

Here,

let me touch your fingertips.

It was there

I first found the only hint.

forgotten dreams

Love came down at Christmas
and knelt on one knee,
the other one poised
on the edge of anticipation.
It took some music,
and it took a lot of little lights
cast around the room,
flung like dandelion seeds
by the breath of a delighted child,
but that seemed to be enough,
and soon there was the silence
of astonishment all over again.

After that,
some darkness had diminished,
and there was some holding close,
and off in the distance
a train whistle blew,
proclaiming peace.

Sadness slept,
deep and undisturbed.

In the morning,
even lost socks
elicited laughter,
whimsical and clear,
and all was well again.
You could almost imagine
that the whole world
had turned over a new leaf
and forgotten
whatever the fight
was all about anyway.

requiem

I came here looking for Mozart.
I wanted to dip my bucket
into the deep well
from which he pulled
all that *lux perpetua*
and feel the tremors
of all those insistent
dies iraes and illas.
I wanted to quake where he quaked,
soar where he soared,
remember something
that happened before I was born.

But I had to find a way to eat.
They gave me a horn
someone had left backstage
when the circus
had to bolt and run last month
and said
surely I could give them some Sousa
in return for their euros –
I was an American, after all.

I asked them to show me
where the thrift shop was.
The jacket
smells a little sour under the arms,
but the sleeves are the right length.
No one wears stripes any more,
which is why
there were so many of them.

I found the ace in the pocket.
I might need it some time;
there are many ways to make a living,
not all of them gnarly.
I miss my wife.

I gave her *Eine Kleine Nachtmusik*
for her ring.
That way, when she calls,
I remember something
that will happen again
after I get home.

She says the baby
is moving a lot by now,
and is squeezing
all the breath out of her.
She says she will sing again later.

I also miss my jeans.
There is nothing better
than a good pair of jeans.
Well, almost nothing.
Let's see,
if I want to take a picture
with this thing
I have to. . . um. . .

By the way,
the Cathedral Choir
is doing the *Ave Verum Corpus*
over the lunch hour today.
You're welcome to come along.
But I have to warn you:
I might cry.
Are you the kind of person
who would understand why?

annunciation

Now what?
I'm looking out there,
trying to see what you see.
Trying to understand
how it is you will accomplish
the turning-upside-down
of this world,
the bringing up to the top
all those down there,
the toppling of these peaks.

Still, this fluttering in my belly
tells me
my first instinct about you
was right.
You can do
what you say you will.
You are
who I think you are.

a slice of americana

Warm summer evenings.
The porch still has a swing
and the park still has sandlot ball.
There's nothing to frighten,
nothing to mourn.

There's no one to tell you
you aren't beautiful,
no one to tell you you *can't*.

You don't know a stranger.
There's nothing you need to buy,
and your grandpa still comes over
with a pocketknife
and a piece of willow.
When he is done
teaching you how to whittle,
he will teach you how to whistle
with what you've made.

You can't imagine
the worse that can happen,
but even if you could,
it never occurs to you
that it might happen to you.

You catch fireflies at dusk
and put them in a Ball jar
with a bent lid
and poke holes in the top
with an ice pick
so the bugs can breathe,
and the jar is your lantern
as you pick cicada shells off the elm tree
by the curb where the popsicle truck
is just now pulling up to a stop.
You think it is because you have blue eyes
that you like the blueberry ices the best.

You hate it when your mother
calls you to come in,
but at least you have Nancy Drew
and The Hardy Boys
to keep you company under the covers
after all the lights are out
and you pull out the flashlight
you hid under your pillow
when you made the bed in the morning,
the one you think your mother
knows nothing about.

Your father's stubbled face tickles you
when he bends to kiss you goodnight,
and sometimes he sings a wordless song
low under his breath
until the next thing you know
it is morning again.

Your grandma still uses lard for the crust
and green apples
from the ancient gnarled tree
out back by the chokecherry bush,
and it bores you to death to sit inside
in front of a video screen of any sort.

You still like the fact that you look alike
and you can't really remember the last time
you felt like pinching each other,
and you share your allowance
to buy the big things
you couldn't afford on your own
and you always give some
to Tommy down the street
whose father is not like your father,
and you have never been gladder
of anything in your life.

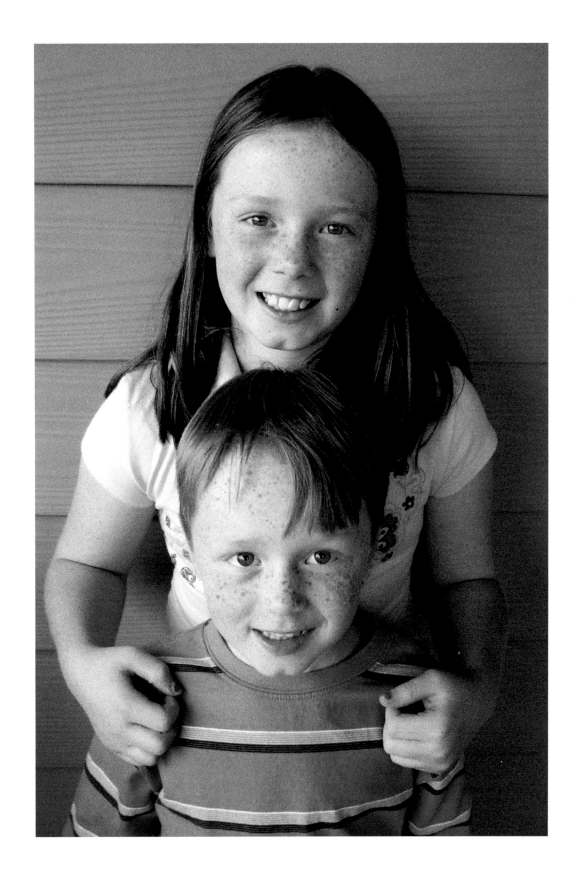

you take my breath away

the music
of the spheres

until I can no longer sing

but only listen

and disintegrate

in joy

well woman

I don't know what you see in me.

Heat, color, dirt, sweat.

These drapes, found.

This cup, not mine.

I work for a living.

Go ahead, sneer.

I tried marriage,

but it bruised me.

Tell me I am not worthy.

Tell me I am useless.

There are many

who do not think so.

They leave their trails

in the dust of my memory,

etched and aching.

I am always thirsty.

Now, you, here.

Like something out of a dream.

Looking at me that way,

knowing I have no name.

Someone called me Dulcinea once,

but he rode off

in a storm of scorn,

fighting visions he did not ask for,

desires he could not answer.

Name me not.

I am not yours.

But then,

neither do you belong here,

near me,

soaking in this sorrow.

Still, say it again.

That you are all I'll ever need.

That I am done

with slinking around

in the heat of the day.

That people will

listen to me, to *me*.

*missing
in action*

Where'd he go?

I don't know!
He was here a minute ago.

Well, he can't have gone far.

Augh!
What if he fell in and drowned?

He didn't drown!
I taught him to swim myself.
There's no way
he would have drowned!

Well, where is he then?
The lake is so still.
There are no ripples anywhere,
nothing,
not even a whisper of wind
ruffling the surface.

There's someone on the shore
over there,
just getting ready
to start the day.
Let's go ask him!
He might have seen something.

Hey! You, there!
Did you see someone
come in from this boat here?
Did you see someone
swim to shore?

No? Well, thanks anyway.

Hey.
Come here.
Give me your hand.
Feel that?
The cushion is still warm.
He can't have been gone long.
Come on!
We'll find him.
Come on!
Hurry up!

But the lake!
It is so still, so beautiful.
You go on ahead.
I'll be right there.
I just want to sit here
and look at the lake
a little while longer,
just a little while longer.

the decline
of faith

There are many ways
you can separate in from out,
light from dark.

Walls work very well,
especially when
you give over your beauty to them,
all the sweet newness
flowing around inside you
like ribbons,
and then trace
lyrical designs upon them
until they shine with grace.

The thing is,
even if they are
the most beautiful walls
you have ever built
in your entire life,
people will still walk by them
and not notice they are there.
Most people will do this,
as a matter of fact,
and never realize
the danger of it at all.
More of them than you imagine
will never bother to wonder
whether it is good or evil
that shimmers in secrecy
under the ripe dome.

You must be satisfied
with the one old woman –
or if you are lucky, two –
looking down instead of up,
looking into the ordinary
to find something
sacramental enough
to take inside,
where the incense of it
and the ashes of it,
burnt in holiness and hope,
will rise like birdsong
on the air of dawn.

Some of them cried out for joy,

tired of harboring ancient chants,

but others keened their anguished wait

long into the night,

raking the ears

of babies and old women

until they shut them up

with tears of their own.

stones falling

Some, when they fell, shattered.

Others rolled away into little heaps

where bright boys picked them up

and practiced their fort-building

and their weapon-slinging

until they felt like men.

Some hang on, expecting

they know not what.

I'm going home now.

I have a family to feed,

and I have stood

about as much loneliness

as anyone can be expected to stand.

But call me when your watch is over,

no matter what the hour of the day.

I want to be here

when the trumpet sounds.

brothers

Before you go chasing after speed,

before you understand your bloodlust

for what it is,

the havoc it can reap,

before your hormones

override your higher brain function

even in moments of seeming lucidity,

before you invent

the next generation of tools

or set the record

for the highest score ever,

or buy low

and sell twice as high as you ought to

and swamp the competition,

completely swamp them,

stop.

Remember what it felt like to be small,

and to look a lot like somebody else,

and to be soft without being weak.

Remember how easy it was to trust

that somebody who loved you

had your back,

and how good it felt

to be free and unafraid

and as yet unscarred.

Remember that

art is as powerful as annihilation

when it comes to

getting someone's attention.

Remember that bread can make peace

when it is passed around.

Remember that even the tiniest children

seem to want to look you straight in the eye.

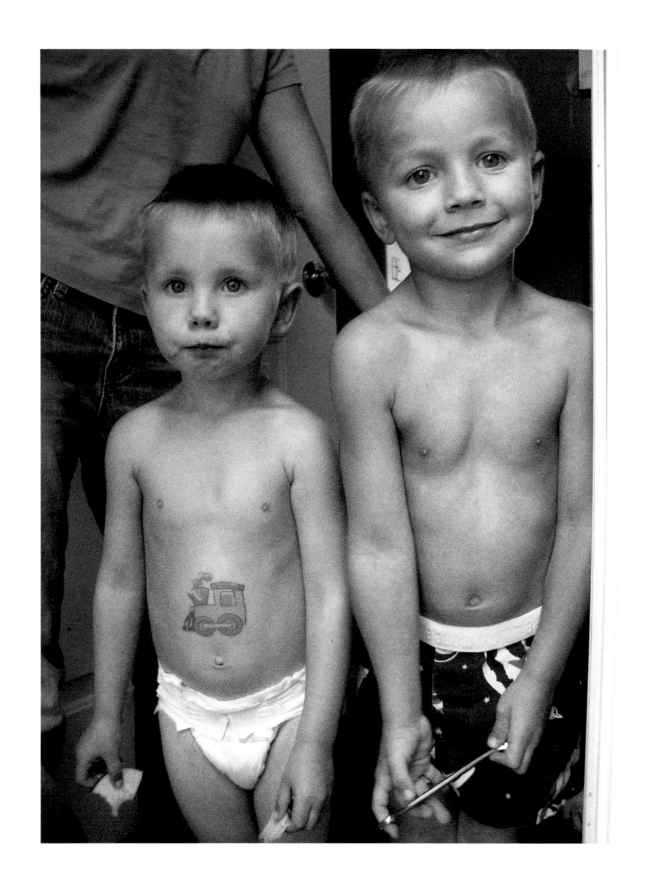

happy trails

Chaps of red leather
hide farrier's tools.
Wind in the willows
sings loudly of fools.

Buffalo wait,
oblivious still.
Heat rises silently
over the hills.

Long years in the saddle,
long years underneath,
have taught them to lean,
taught them to breathe.

The horse and the man
have held gaze before this.
Still, trust is a thing
you must never dismiss.

So, come along boys,
no more contemplating.
Be swift and be true;
there's action awaiting!

One needs a hand,
the other a hunt.
There's no need to fear,
no need to confront.

grace

You can tell
when the sogginess and sorrow
are about to lift.
Something makes you turn
so the light is behind you now,
so you can see that the spectre
that has been haunting you since dawn
is merely your own shadow,
ludicrous and magnified.

Now you know:
the call of the riptide
is not the only future set for you.
You do not have to drown after all.
You can,
feet still firmly grounded
in the life-saving sand,
lean into that other music
that is not the ocean's
moaning, booming bass.
Lean full-bodied
into that other flute-filled arc,
that light ripple of white
that holds its blue
the way the sky holds its day.

lament

There is such a thing
as too much light.
Think of the night sky
above a sprawling mall-loving horde,
incessantly bright
and artificially consistent.
Remember before that,
when night was dark
unless spangled by stars
or by the looming orb of moon,
lathering the lake
with something like iridescent lace.
Think of dark deep enough
to stumble in,
and the great glad hint of dawn
that yanks you up and out of fear
when it is, finally, here.
Think of how you can read
each other's eye-light in the gloom
and how the world
becomes a room filled with comfort.

Don't toy with the sky.
You might forget
you are not God.

Index